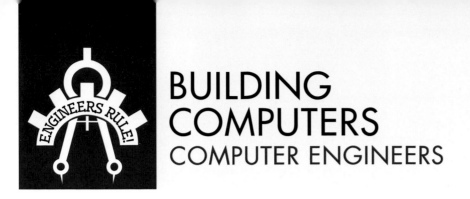

BUILDING COMPUTERS
COMPUTER ENGINEERS

DANIEL R. FAUST

PowerKiDS press

New York

Published in 2016 by The Rosen Publishing Group, Inc.
29 East 21st Street, New York, NY 10010

First Edition

Editor: Caitlin McAneney
Book Design: Katelyn Heinle

Library of Congress Cataloging-in-Publication Data

Faust, Daniel R., author.
 Building computers : computer engineers / Daniel R. Faust.
    pages cm — (Engineers rule!)
 Includes bibliographical references and index.
 ISBN 978-1-5081-4536-3 (pbk.)
 ISBN 978-1-5081-4537-0 (6 pack)
 ISBN 978-1-5081-4538-7 (library binding)
 1. Electronic digital computers—Design and construction—Juvenile literature. I. Title.
 TK7885.5.F38 2016
 004—dc23
                              2015026677

Manufactured in the United States of America

CPSIA Compliance Information: Batch #BW16PK: For Further Information contact Rosen Publishing, New York, New York at 1-800-237-9932

CONTENTS

Life in the Computer Age 4

What Is a Computer Engineer? 6

Tools of the Trade 8

Amazing Math Machines. 10

The First Computers. 12

The Colossus. 14

The U.S. Navy and MIT 16

NASA Needs Computers 18

Computer Engineering Specialties. 20

To Serve and Protect. 22

Lights! Cameras! Computers! 24

To Mars and Beyond 26

Becoming a Computer Engineer 28

Tomorrow's Computer Engineers 30

Glossary 31

Index. 32

Websites 32

LIFE IN THE COMPUTER AGE

Computers are all around us. You probably use computers at school and at home. Your parents probably use them at work, too. Power companies use computers to keep the electricity running in houses and businesses. Computers help cars and airplanes get where they're going. With laptops, tablets, smartphones, and smartwatches, computers are getting small enough that you can take them anywhere.

It might be hard to imagine a world without computers. However, there was a time not long ago when there wasn't a computer in every home and office. Modern computers exist only because of the **innovative** men and women who helped invent, design, improve, and build these amazing machines. Without computer engineers, our lives would be very different than they are today.

Computers have become an important part of our everyday lives. Have you ever stopped to think about the engineers who design the computers you use?

WHAT IS A COMPUTER ENGINEER?

The men and women responsible for creating the computers we use every day are called computer engineers. Computer engineering combines skills from different fields of study, such as electrical engineering and computer science. Computer engineers research, develop, design, and test different computer equipment. Some computer engineers improve existing equipment. They try to make it more **efficient** or able to work with newer **software**. Other engineers design new equipment or **firmware**.

Computer engineers are responsible for designing the key components—or parts—of computers, such as microcontrollers, microprocessors, circuit boards, and operating systems. Most computer engineers work for research laboratories or manufacturing companies. Some computer engineers find work with the federal government. As our society continues to advance with technology, computer engineering will be one of the most important jobs of the future.

Computer engineers design every part of a computer. If anyone knows a computer inside and out, it's a computer engineer.

INTEGRATED CIRCUIT
A VERY SMALL ELECTRONIC
CIRCUIT MADE UP OF SEVERAL
ELECTRONIC COMPONENTS;
ALSO CALLED A MICROCHIP

CIRCUIT BOARD
A SHEET USED FOR MOUNTING
AND CONNECTING ELECTRONIC
COMPONENTS

COMPUTER COMPONENTS

MICROCONTROLLER
A SMALL COMPUTER BUILT
ON AN INTEGRATED
CIRCUIT

MICROPROCESSOR
A SINGLE INTEGRATED CIRCUIT
PERFORMING THE BASIC FUNCTIONS
OF THE CENTRAL PROCESSING UNIT, OR
DEVICE THAT EXECUTES INSTRUCTIONS
FROM THE SOFTWARE

OPERATING SYSTEM
THE SOFTWARE THAT MANAGES
COMPUTER HARDWARE
AND SOFTWARE

MOTHERBOARD
A SLOTTED BOARD USED TO
HOLD MULTIPLE CIRCUIT BOARDS

TOOLS OF THE TRADE

Computer engineering is an exciting and rewarding field of study, but it takes a lot of time and hard work. It usually takes between four and seven years of college to become a qualified computer engineer. Computer engineers need to be detail oriented, possess excellent problem-solving skills, and be able to manage their time efficiently. Computer engineering students study engineering techniques, mathematics, electronics, and computer programming.

Computer engineers learn how to use a number of different tools and programs. Multimeters, tester screwdrivers, and logic probes are used to examine and test delicate computer circuits. Wire cutters, strippers, and soldering irons are used to repair damaged computer parts. Engineers use design software to **render** designs for circuits, chips, and other hardware.

Like other careers, computer engineers use special tools to do their job. These tools help them test and repair the delicate parts of a computer.

HOW THE DIFFERENT PARTS OF A COMPUTER INTERACT

INPUT: Input is a way of getting information into your computer that it can process. Ways of input include a keyboard and mouse.

PROCESSOR: The central processing unit, or CPU, is your computer's brain. It does all the calculations necessary for the computer to work.

MEMORY/STORAGE: Your computer stores documents and files on a hard drive or on portable flash memory drives.

OUTPUT: This is how your computer displays information. Information can be displayed on a screen or as a permanent copy produced by a printer.

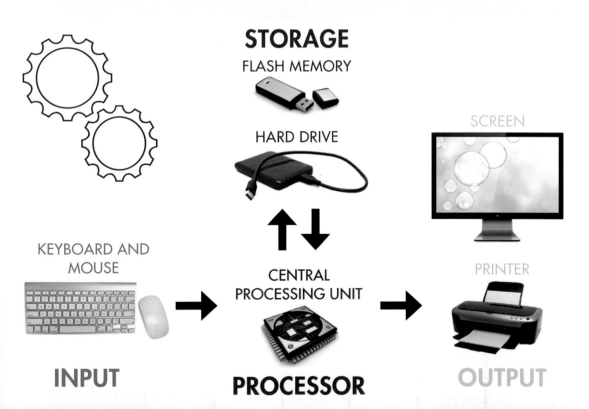

STORAGE

FLASH MEMORY

HARD DRIVE

SCREEN

KEYBOARD AND MOUSE

CENTRAL PROCESSING UNIT

PRINTER

INPUT

PROCESSOR

OUTPUT

AMAZING MATH MACHINES

Long before computers, people relied on printed tables of numbers to perform anything but the simplest mathematical calculations. These tables were often copied and printed by hand, meaning it was possible—even likely—for errors to appear. An incorrect calculation could spell disaster for an engineer, architect, or navigator. In 1821, mathematician and inventor Charles Babbage came up with an idea for a machine that could perform calculations without error.

The machine Babbage invented was called the Difference Engine. The Difference Engine used a series of rotating parts to perform calculations. Babbage also invented the more **complex** Analytical Engine. The Analytical Engine was a lot like your modern computer in many ways. It was programmable, could perform multiple mathematical functions, and could provide output in different formats, such as punched cards and graphs.

ADA LOVELACE

ADA LOVELACE (1815–1852)

Ada Lovelace was the daughter of poet Lord Byron and a gifted mathematician. Lovelace was tutored in science and mathematics from a young age. When she was about 17, she met Charles Babbage and saw his Difference Engine. Later, Lovelace created an **algorithm** that allowed Babbage's Analytical Engine to handle letters and symbols as well as numbers. Many of her ideas are used in modern computing. For this reason, Ada Lovelace is often considered the first computer programmer.

DIFFERENCE ENGINE

Babbage was never able to build a working version of his Difference Engine. Using Babbage's original designs, the Science Museum in London completed a working Difference Engine in 2002.

THE FIRST COMPUTERS

Maybe you've seen pictures of the first cars, televisions, and telephones. They don't look like the cars, televisions, and telephones we use today. As technology advances, designers and engineers change and improve existing devices. That's what happened to computers, too.

The first computers were large machines. Some even took up entire rooms! These earliest computers were giant calculators, and they were used to solve lengthy and complicated math problems more quickly and accurately than a human could. The first computers were controlled using **electromagnetic** switches called relays and vacuum tubes, which are glass tubes used to conduct electricity. Although they could perform tasks faster than a person, the first computers were very slow compared to modern computers.

> Technology is constantly changing. Like cars and telephones, the earliest computers are almost unrecognizable compared to modern computers.

THE COLOSSUS

During World War II, both sides used codes to send important messages. If one side could find a way to **decrypt** the other side's codes, they would gain a huge advantage. Both the British and American governments worked hard to decrypt the codes used by their enemies in Europe and the Pacific. The British code breakers operated from Bletchley Park—an estate in southeast England.

The German code machines were famous for producing codes that were difficult to decrypt. To help break these codes, the British code breakers relied on ten Colossus computers. Engineer Tommy Flowers designed and built the first Colossus in 1943. The Colossus used switches and vacuum tubes to perform counting and searching operations. Many consider it the first large-scale, programmable, electronic computer.

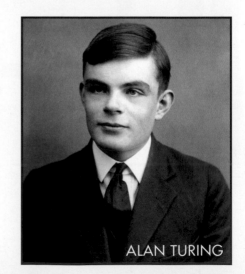

ALAN TURING

ALAN TURING

Born in 1912, Englishman Alan Turing is considered by many to be the father of modern computer science. One of Turing's earliest works proposed the idea of a universal machine that would be able to compute anything. The "Turing machine" became the foundation for the concept of the modern computer. During World War II, Turing was one of the leading code breakers working at Bletchley Park. After the war, he helped design the Automatic Computing Engine (ACE), which influenced the design of the world's first personal computer.

COLOSSUS

The original Colossus computers were destroyed after the war to maintain the project's secrecy. A model of the Colossus was completed in 2007 and is on display at Bletchley Park.

THE U.S. NAVY AND MIT

During World War II, the U.S. Navy was interested in creating a computer that could be used as a flight **simulator** to train bomber crews. Engineers at the Massachusetts Institute of Technology, or MIT, attempted to build such a computer, which the U.S. Navy called Project Whirlwind. Unfortunately, the original computer was incapable of performing the number of tasks the navy required.

The MIT engineers realized they needed a machine that was faster, more accurate, and more complex. Instead of building a larger machine, they decided they needed a better computer. At the time, computers could only be programmed to perform a single task. Whirlwind needed to be able to perform an ever-changing series of tasks. Whirlwind's ability to be programmed to perform more than one task at a time helped pave the way for later business and personal computers.

Does this look like a computer to you? Vacuum tubes like these were an important part of early computers like the Whirlwind.

16

VACUUM TUBES

NASA NEEDS COMPUTERS

In 1969, NASA successfully landed astronauts on the moon. That single event changed the course of space exploration. It also led to rapid technological advancements, especially in the fields of electronics and computing. NASA needed computers that were more powerful than the ones that existed at the time. They also needed computers that were smaller and lighter than the computers that were available, leading to the development of the microchip and the microprocessor.

Microprocessors made it cheaper and easier to build computers. Companies like Commodore, IBM, and Apple were able to take advantage of new technology and started selling small, inexpensive computers—called personal computers (PCs)—to consumers. These companies relied on computer engineers to make improvements that would help their computers stand out from the rest.

The earliest PCs available to the public were sold as kits that had to be built at home. Eventually, anyone could buy prebuilt models, such as this Altair 8800.

ALTAIR 8800

When you think about all the different kinds of computers in the world, it should come as no surprise that there are many different specialties in the field of computer engineering. Because almost every industry has become dependent on computer technology, computer engineers have the opportunity to work in a wide range of different industries, like transportation, science, medicine, and the military.

Computers have played a role in code breaking since the days of World War II and continue to do so today. Some engineers specialize in designing and improving communications and wireless networks. Other engineers work on designing reliable, high-performance computers and computer components. Computer engineers can also specialize in cybersecurity, mobile computing, and **nanotechnology**, while others focus on green computing.

Some computer engineers specialize in parallel computing, or using multiple computers, like these supercomputers, to perform many calculations at the same time.

WHAT IS GREEN COMPUTING?

Green computing is the intersection between computer engineering and **environmentalism**. Green computing tries to find environmentally friendly approaches to making computers. These engineers try to improve energy efficiency by minimizing the amount of energy used by computers. Then they design computers and other digital devices that are energy efficient. Some find ways to limit waste during the manufacturing of computers and other digital devices. Other engineers work on recycling parts of existing computers or finding safe, eco-friendly ways to dispose of unwanted devices.

TO SERVE AND PROTECT

Since the days of the first computers, the U.S. military has relied on these machines to train soldiers, improve weapon accuracy, and keep an eye on the enemy. Today, computer engineers work for all branches of the military, as well as intelligence and law enforcement agencies such as the CIA, NSA, and FBI.

The military and government constantly need better and more powerful computers for secure communications, information gathering, and data analysis. Like your family car, computers are key components in military **vehicles**, such as jet fighters, tanks, and aircraft carriers. The men and women who watch our skies use radar systems that rely on advanced computers. The drones—or unmanned aircraft—used by the military need computers to function properly. In recent years, computer engineers have had to fight and guard against cybercriminals and hackers.

Hackers and other cybercriminals steal information from people online, including private messages and bank account information. Computer engineers working for law enforcement are designing ways to keep our information safe.

OCKED

Password write.

LIGHTS! CAMERAS! COMPUTERS!

Do you like to play video games? You can bet computer engineers had a hand in designing and building your favorite gaming system. Computer engineers also work behind the scenes of your favorite movies and television shows and even at your local theme park.

We've come to expect mind-blowing special effects in our movies, but did you ever stop to think about the technology behind them? Computer engineers had to design the computers used to create all the digital effects we see in movies. Computer engineers are also responsible for designing the computers used to control cameras and edit film. Special-effects skills can also be applied to designing rides and attractions at theme parks such as Universal Studios, Six Flags, and Disney World.

Countless movies and video games use motion capture, or mocap, technology. Computer engineers needed to design and create the computers used in this process.

TO MARS AND BEYOND

Computers are still an important part of NASA's space exploration mission, and computer engineers are still important players in these missions. Computer engineers design, develop, test, and evaluate new computer systems used in NASA's aircraft, spacecraft, and support equipment.

Imagine the calculations needed to launch a spacecraft from Earth and land it on Mars or an asteroid floating in deep space. Only a computer could do that. NASA's needs frequently require it to seek out faster, more powerful computers. Giant computers crunch numbers, while technicians at computer terminals track the movement of satellites and other objects. When NASA plans missions to Mars and other planets, it needs computer engineers to design computers that are tough enough to survive in the harsh environments of deep space and other planets.

Computer engineers who work for NASA have an interesting problem that engineers in other fields never face—designing computers that can survive on other planets.

BECOMING A COMPUTER ENGINEER

Do you like using computers? Are you interested in how machines work? If so, a career as a computer engineer might be perfect for you. How can you land a career in this exciting field?

First, make sure to pay attention in your science, technology, engineering, and math classes. All these subjects are important in computer engineering. Your school or community center may even offer extra computer science and coding classes. Someday, you'll need at least a bachelor's degree in computer engineering or a related field, such as computer science or mathematics. After that, you can either keep going to school for an advanced degree or start an entry-level job. You can choose to specialize in one aspect of computer engineering, such as hardware or software.

Computer engineers have to study for many years to understand how to design and create new computer hardware.

Thirty years ago, smartphones and tablets only existed in science fiction movies. Today, not only are they real, but people use them every day. What kinds of new technologies will tomorrow's computer engineers create? Computers are already small enough to fit in your pocket and on your wrist. Could the future see a computer small enough to fit on the tip of your finger?

Computer engineers are already working on new ways to input and display information. Imagine a future where your computer keyboard and screen are simply projections you can physically interact with. Engineers are also researching how to make computers that can recognize a person's emotional state based on facial expressions and body posture. Some are even working on self-driving cars. Computer engineers hold the key to our future!

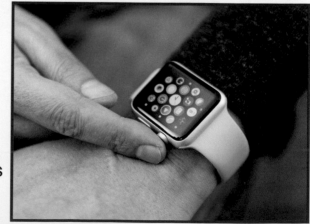

GLOSSARY

algorithm: A set of steps that are followed in order to solve a mathematical problem or complete a computer process.

complex: Not easy to understand or explain. Also, having to do with something with many parts that work together.

decrypt: To decode.

efficient: Done in the quickest, best way possible.

electromagnetic: Relating to the magnetic field that's produced by a current of electricity.

environmentalism: A movement to preserve, restore, and improve the natural world.

firmware: Coded instructions that are permanently stored in a computer's memory.

innovative: Using or showing new methods or ideas.

nanotechnology: The science and technology of devices and materials constructed on extremely small scales.

render: To produce a visual representation of something.

simulator: A laboratory device that reproduces conditions and events likely to occur in real life.

software: Programs that run on computers and perform certain functions.

vehicle: An object used for carrying or transporting people or goods.

INDEX

A
ACE, 15
Analytical Engine, 10, 11

B
Babbage, Charles, 10, 11
Bletchley Park, 14, 15

C
circuit boards, 6, 7
classes, 28
code breakers, 14, 15, 20
college, 8
Colossus computers, 14, 15
CPU, 9
cybercriminals, 22

D
Difference Engine, 10, 11

F
firmware, 6
Flowers, Tommy, 14

H
hackers, 22
hardware, 7, 8, 28

I
input, 9, 30
integrated circuit, 7

L
Lovelace, Ada, 10, 11

M
memory/storage, 9
microchip, 7, 18
microcontrollers, 6, 7
microprocessors, 6, 7, 18
military, 20, 22
motherboard, 7
movies, 24, 25, 30

N
NASA, 18, 26, 27

O
operating systems, 6, 7
output, 9, 10

P
personal computer, 15, 16, 18
processor, 9
programs, 8
Project Whirlwind, 16

S
skills, 6, 8, 24
software, 6, 7, 8, 28
specialties, 20

T
theme parks, 24
tools, 8
Turing, Alan, 14, 15

V
video games, 24, 25

WEBSITES

Due to the changing nature of Internet links, PowerKids Press has developed an online list of websites related to the subject of this book. This site is updated regularly. Please use this link to access the list: www.powerkidslinks.com/engin/comp